101 Life-Changing
Latin Proverbs

Wisdom from Ancient Rome,
Translated and Explained

101 Life-Changing Latin Proverbs: *Wisdom from Ancient Rome, Translated and Explained*

© [16/06/2025] [Maxwell W. Wilson]

Cover design by Timothy Brooks

ISBN: [9798288222382]

Disclaimer : *This book is for informational purposes only. While every effort has been made to ensure the accuracy and completeness of the information contained herein, the author and publisher assume no responsibility for errors, inaccuracies, omissions, or any outcomes resulting from the use of this information. The content is provided on an "as-is" basis and does not constitute professional or technical advice. Readers are encouraged to consult official sources and professionals for specific guidance.*

Trademarks : *All brand names and product names used in this book are trademarks, registered trademarks, or trade names of their respective holders. The use of trademarks is for reference only and does not imply any affiliation with or endorsement by the trademark holders.*

For permissions, media inquiries, or publishing opportunities, please contact the author at: sspider1012@gmail.com

Incipe audacter: fortuna iuvat fortes.

To the thinkers who question,
the seekers who reflect,
and the quiet souls who carry ancient
wisdom into a noisy world.

And to Rome—
not just the city or the empire,
but the idea
that words can outlive walls,
and that virtue is still worth striving for.

The ancient Romans built empires of stone, but their words—sharpened by war, philosophy, politics, and poetry—have outlasted their monuments. This book is a curated collection of 101 proverbs born from the heart of Roman civilization: words that shaped the moral codes of empires, whispered wisdom to generals and emperors, and echoed through the centuries into courtrooms, classrooms, and quiet personal moments of reflection.

These proverbs are not mere relics of a distant past. They are mirrors. They reflect what it meant—and still means—to live with discipline, ambition, courage, honor, and restraint. Some lines are fierce and stern, carved from the Stoic bedrock of Roman philosophy. Others are lyrical, poetic, even tender. But all of them contain something rare in our world today: clarity. Clarity of thought, of consequence, of human nature.

Each saying in this book appears in its original Latin—both as a nod to its heritage and as an invitation to listen to the rhythm and brevity the Romans mastered. Below that, you'll find a modern English translation followed by a brief interpretation. These aren't academic footnotes; they're meant to be companions—guides for applying ancient wisdom to modern life. This is not a history book, though you'll find history between the lines. It's not a language textbook, though Latin breathes through every page. It is, instead, a book of deep thought, distilled into compact wisdom. It is for thinkers, dreamers, builders, writers, students, and anyone who's ever looked for a compass in a complicated world.

May these 101 proverbs serve you not just as insights—but as tools. May they challenge and inspire, comfort and correct, illuminate and endure. After all, *verba volant, scripta manent*—spoken words fly away, but the written word remains

Fortes fortuna adiuvat
Fortune favors the brave.
The Romans admired boldness. Whether on the battlefield or in political life, they believed that luck was not random—it smiled upon those who dared to act decisively.

Memento mori
Remember that you will die.
Not a morbid warning, but a profound call to live well. By keeping death close in thought, one is sharpened to live more deliberately, with humility and urgency.

Quidquid agis, prudenter agas et respice finem
Whatever you do, do wisely and consider the end.
Wisdom, for the Romans, meant foresight. This proverb urges thoughtful action—never just for the moment, but always with an eye on where it leads.

Aquila non capit muscas
The eagle does not catch flies.
Great souls don't waste energy on petty concerns. This sharp metaphor reminds us to rise above trivialities and act with the dignity of our true stature.

Fiat voluntas tua
Let your will be done.
Beyond religious origins, this became a Roman affirmation of inner strength. It reflects the power of will to shape reality, even in the face of resistance.

Mens sana in corpore sano
A sound mind in a sound body.
The ideal Roman citizen cultivated both intellect and strength. Mental clarity and physical health were inseparable virtues in their pursuit of excellence.

Si vis pacem, para bellum
If you want peace, prepare for war.
Lasting peace requires readiness. This was not just military doctrine, but a life principle: peace is preserved not by passivity, but by strength held in restraint.

Nil desperandum
Never despair.
A defiant piece of Stoic optimism. No matter the loss or difficulty, this phrase was a call to hold firm. Despair was not just weakness—it was dishonor.

Amat victoria curam
Victory loves careful preparation.
Fortune may play a part, but the Romans knew triumph belonged to the meticulous. Thought, effort, and attention to detail were the real architects of success.

Non ducor, duco
I am not led; I lead.
A declaration of independence and agency. It embodies the Roman ideal of the leader—not a ruler of others, but one who takes full command of self.

Audentes fortuna iuvat
Fortune helps those who dare.
A variation of a familiar theme, but with an emphasis on daring over mere bravery. To dare is to act without guarantee—an ideal deeply embedded in Roman valor.

Faber est suae quisque fortunae
Every man is the architect of his own fortune.
Romans respected destiny, but they revered responsibility more. Your fate is not written in the stars—it is built by your choices, brick by brick.

Dum spiro, spero
While I breathe, I hope.
Hope was not weakness, but a breath-by-breath resilience.
As long as life endures, so too does the possibility of
transformation.

In vino veritas
In wine, there is truth.
Spoken with both wit and caution, this reminds us how
facades drop in moments of vulnerability. Sometimes,
sincerity slips through the cracks of control.

Verba volant, scripta manent
Spoken words fly away, written ones remain.
The Romans were a civilization of law, literature, and
legacy. This proverb teaches the enduring weight of
writing—its power to outlast memory.

Dura lex, sed lex
The law is harsh, but it is the law.
A nod to the Roman obsession with order. Justice may be
strict, even cruel, but the structure it brings is better than
chaos.

Tempus fugit
Time flies.
A reminder of impermanence. For the Romans, time was not a river to be waded in, but a storm that carried us forward—swift, relentless, irreversible.

Vita brevis, ars longa
Life is short, art is long.
Art, wisdom, and knowledge outlive their creators. Our work—if crafted well—becomes our immortality.

Divide et impera
Divide and conquer.
Though often political, it speaks to a broader strategy: break complexity into parts to master it. Control, even of the self, begins with intelligent separation.

Caveat emptor
Let the buyer beware.
A practical warning in commerce and in life. Responsibility lies with the one who chooses—vigilance is part of survival.

Carpe diem
Seize the day.
Immortalized by Horace, this is not an invitation to recklessness but a call to presence. Life is fleeting—embrace what is now before it fades.

Acta, non verba
Deeds, not words.
Romans measured worth not by speech but by action. Talk may impress, but it is action that builds roads, wins battles, and changes lives.

Gladiator in arena consilium capit
The gladiator makes his plan in the arena.
It's easy to theorize, but real decisions come under pressure. This speaks to adaptability—the wisdom that arises not in calm, but in the heat of struggle.

Ars est celare artem
True art is to conceal art.
Mastery hides effort. The most profound works appear simple, seamless—as if they simply "are." A lesson in grace and restraint.

Homo homini lupus est
Man is a wolf to man.

A stark reflection on human nature. Without laws and virtue, people may become each other's worst enemy. Civilization is a fragile shield.

Fortuna caeca est
Fortune is blind.

Luck plays no favorites. The Romans knew that wealth and ruin both come uninvited. Therefore, character—not chance—is the only true foundation.

Res, non verba
Results, not rhetoric.

A sterner cousin of "acta non verba." What matters in the end is what has been accomplished—not what was promised, imagined, or loudly declared.

Silentium est aureum
Silence is golden.

Speech may be silver, but silence—well-timed and intentional—is wisdom itself. In the Roman court, battlefield, and home, silence often said the most.

Lux et veritas
Light and truth.
Often paired, for one reveals the other. This is a quiet
anthem for clarity—both moral and intellectual—amidst
the fog of deception and illusion.

Labor omnia vincit
Work conquers all.
This was not just a slogan—it was Rome. Through roads,
walls, aqueducts, and empires, the Romans believed sheer
effort could shape the world.

Natura non facit saltus
Nature does not make leaps.
Change is gradual. Growth, decay, healing—none happen
overnight. The Roman mind admired patience and the
rhythm of natural progress.

Audire est operae pretium
It is worth the trouble to listen.
True wisdom begins with listening. In courts, councils, and
life, understanding came first through attentive ears, not
impulsive tongues.

Ubi concordia, ibi victoria
Where there is unity, there is victory.
Success follows solidarity. From armies to Senate, Rome thrived when people stood together with shared purpose.

Civis Romanus sum
I am a Roman citizen.
More than a legal identity, this was a declaration of dignity and belonging. Citizenship meant rights, responsibility, and honor.

Omnium rerum principia parva sunt
The beginnings of all things are small.
Every empire starts with a single village, every tree with a seed. Nothing grand emerges fully formed—humble origins are the rule, not the exception.

Virtus tentamine gaudet
Virtue rejoices in trial.
Strength of character grows through difficulty. Without challenge, there is no refinement—only the illusion of virtue.

Sine ira et studio

Without anger and bias.

An ideal of Roman historians: truth should be told calmly, without personal agenda. A reminder to seek clarity over passion in judgment.

Non scholae sed vitae discimus

We learn not for school, but for life.

Roman education was never just academic—it was practical, preparing citizens to act with intelligence, ethics, and resilience.

Repetitio mater studiorum est

Repetition is the mother of learning.

Mastery comes through rhythm, not revelation. Romans believed that excellence—military or intellectual—was earned through discipline.

Ignorantia legis neminem excusat

Ignorance of the law excuses no one.

You are still responsible, even if unaware. Justice depends on accountability, not innocence through neglect.

Bis vincit qui se vincit in victoria
He conquers twice who conquers himself in victory.
Pride is the final enemy. True triumph is measured by
restraint and humility when power is already in your
hands.

Auctoritas non veritas facit legem
Authority, not truth, makes the law.
A realistic, even cynical observation. Law reflects power,
not always justice. A reminder to remain ethically alert,
even under legal rule.

Post nubila, phoebus
After the clouds, the sun.
Light returns. Suffering fades. This elegant phrase offered
hope in times of storm—reminding Romans that hardship,
too, passes.

Nullum magnum ingenium sine mixtura dementiae fuit
*There has been no great genius without a touch of
madness.*
Rome acknowledged that brilliance often walked the edge
of reason. Visionaries defy norms—and sometimes, sanity.

Discendo discimus

By teaching, we learn.

The Romans knew that mastery deepened when shared. Explanation sharpens understanding, and generosity fosters clarity.

Nemo sibi nascitur

No one is born for oneself alone.

Community over ego. Even in a world of heroes and emperors, Romans understood the self must serve the whole.

Fiat lux

Let there be light.

Used in poetry, philosophy, and religion, this phrase celebrates the beginning of understanding, knowledge, and renewal.

Crescit sub pondere virtus

Virtue grows beneath burdens.

Character isn't built in ease but under weight. Pressure and pain don't break the soul—they forge it.

Aliquid stat pro aliquo
Something stands for something else.
The roots of symbolism. Romans were acutely aware that signs, tokens, and rituals carried hidden meaning and power.

Mala herba cito crescit
Bad weeds grow quickly.
Evil often spreads faster than good. Just as weeds outpace crops, corruption, vice, and error can flourish unless uprooted early.

Corruptio optimi pessima
The corruption of the best is the worst.
When those who are meant to embody virtue fall, their failure is deeper, more dangerous. Romans feared the decay of excellence more than ordinary vice.

Alea iacta est
The die is cast.
Spoken by Julius Caesar as he crossed the Rubicon, this marks the point of no return. Once action begins, there's no turning back—only forward.

Qui desiderat pacem, praeparet bellum
He who desires peace, should prepare for war.
A sterner formulation of the earlier proverb. Peace is not wished into existence—it must be secured with readiness and strength.

Occasio facit furem
Opportunity makes the thief.
People may appear honest, but the chance to do wrong often reveals true character. A warning about both trust and temptation.

Solitudinem faciunt, pacem appellant
They make a desert and call it peace.
A haunting critique of imperialism and conquest. Sometimes, what's called "peace" is merely the silence left after destruction.

Virtus in media stat
Virtue stands in the middle.
Extremes, even of good, lead to imbalance. The Roman ideal was moderation—courage between cowardice and recklessness, generosity between waste and greed.

Nulla tenaci invia est via
No road is impassable to the persistent.
Where persistence goes, obstacles retreat. Romans built literal roads across empires—this proverb reflects their faith in determined effort.

Dum vitant stulti vitia, in contraria currunt
Fools rush from one vice to another while avoiding the first.
Avoiding a mistake is not the same as choosing wisely. In fleeing one flaw, the unwise often fall into another.

Faciam ut mei memineris
I shall do something that will make you remember me.
A bold statement of legacy. The Romans lived for *memoria*—to be remembered not for existence, but for impact.

Imperium sine fine dedi
I have given you an empire without end.
Spoken by Jupiter in Virgil's *Aeneid*, this line became prophecy and national identity. Rome's ambition was not wealth—but eternity.

Lex talionis
The law of retaliation.
Justice as mirrored response—eye for eye, harm for harm.
The Romans debated, refined, and eventually moved
beyond this, but they never forgot its moral symmetry.

Non omnia possumus omnes
We cannot all do everything.
A humbling truth. No one is complete, no one is capable of
all. Even emperors must lean on others.

Amor tussisque non celatur
Love and a cough cannot be hidden.
The heart, like the body, reveals itself. Romans saw that
the passions, however buried, eventually surface.

Felix qui potuit rerum cognoscere causas
*Happy is he who has been able to know the causes of
things.*
From Virgil—true joy lies not in ignorance, but
understanding. Knowledge of why is more powerful than
knowledge of what.

Magna est vis consuetudinis
Great is the power of habit.
Rome was built on repetition, not spontaneity. Habits
shape character—and in time, nations.

Nemo malus felix
No wicked man is truly happy.
Pleasure may surround the unjust, but inner peace evades
them. For Romans, true happiness required inner
harmony, not external gain.

Audi alteram partem
Hear the other side.
Justice begins with listening. Before judgment, before
punishment, the Roman legal system demanded the
unheard be heard.

Gallia est omnis divisa in partes tres
All Gaul is divided into three parts.
The opening of Caesar's *Commentarii*, this line is as much a
lesson in observation as in conquest—clarity, structure,
and division aid understanding.

Panem et circenses
Bread and circuses.
A critique of how empires control the masses—feed them, entertain them, and they won't revolt. A haunting insight into distraction as a tool of power.

Spes ultima dea
Hope is the last goddess.
When all else fades, hope remains. In Roman myth and life, hope was never naïve—it was sacred.

Nemo mortalium omnibus horis sapit
No mortal is wise at all times.
Even the greatest stumble. The Romans knew that wisdom was momentary and fragile—no one is immune to folly forever.

Ubi solitudinem faciunt, pacem appellant
Where they create desolation, they call it peace.
Repeated for emphasis in history, this stark proverb reveals the hypocrisy of conquest dressed as harmony. A mirror held up to empire.

Dum fata sinunt, vivite laeti
While fate allows, live joyfully.
The Stoics respected fate, but they also embraced joy. Life is brief—so while the gods permit, rejoice fully and without shame.

Qui tacet, consentire videtur
He who is silent is taken to agree.
Silence isn't neutral. In law, politics, or morality—if you do not object, you may be counted among the consenting.

Non nobis solum nati sumus
We are not born for ourselves alone.
Life's purpose stretches beyond self-interest. Romans believed duty to others—family, state, mankind—was the true measure of virtue.

Stat sua cuique dies
Each has his appointed day.
No one escapes their destined hour. Whether emperor or peasant, every life has its ending already written by the Fates.

Fac fortia et patere
Do brave deeds and endure.
Courage is not mere action—it is followed by endurance. Romans valued those who could not only act, but withstand.

Fortuna vitrea est: tum cum splendet frangitur
Fortune is like glass: just when it gleams brightest, it shatters.
A haunting image of fragility. The higher you rise, the closer you come to breakage. Rome saw countless examples.

Quam bene vivas refert, non quam diu
It is how well you live that matters, not how long.
Legacy isn't measured in years but in meaning. The Romans pursued *virtus*—not longevity, but honor.

Tantae molis erat Romanam condere gentem
So great was the task of founding the Roman nation.
From Virgil's *Aeneid*, this honors struggle. The birth of anything great requires enormous labor and sacrifice.

Necessitas legem non habet
Necessity knows no law.
In crisis, rules bend. A pragmatic acknowledgment that survival often rewrites the code.

Nulla poena sine lege
No punishment without law.
Foundational to Roman legalism—punishment must follow principle, not passion. Justice requires structure.

Omnia vincit amor
Love conquers all.
From Virgil, this is not sentimental—it's elemental. Love, in all its forms, surpasses even empire and death.

Aliis inserviendo consumor
Consumed in service to others.
A metaphor for devotion. Like a candle that gives light by burning, some live best by giving fully.

Malum quidem nullum esse sine aliquo bono
There is no evil without some good.
Even in hardship, something of value can be found. A Stoic's comfort in life's cruelest moments.

Parva scintilla saepe magnam flamam excitat
A small spark often ignites a great flame.
A whisper becomes a revolution. The Romans knew history turns on moments—tiny, often unnoticed, until the blaze.

Virtus non stemma
Virtue, not pedigree.
Nobility isn't inherited—it is earned. The true elite are those of character, not lineage.

Nulli secundus
Second to none.
More than pride, this was the Roman ideal of excellence. Not better than others—simply unmatched in what you are meant to be.

Ab uno disce omnes
From one, learn all.
A single example—good or bad—can reveal the whole. The wise observe a part to understand the pattern.

Morituri te salutant
Those who are about to die salute you.
Said by gladiators to the emperor, it became a chilling anthem of bravery, fate, and the Roman theater of death.

Fiat voluntas tua

Let your will be done.

A phrase of surrender—to fate, to the gods, to purpose. In Rome, it signified acceptance with dignity rather than resistance with despair.

Mens agitat molem

Mind moves matter.

The physical world bends to intellect. Rome's roads, laws, and empires began as thoughts. The true seat of power is not muscle, but mind.

Caelum non animum mutant qui trans mare currunt

Those who cross the sea change the sky, not their soul.

Travel may change scenery, but not the self. Your inner world follows wherever you go. Self-transformation, not relocation, is the true journey.

Lex iniusta non est lex

An unjust law is not law.

The foundation of civil disobedience long before it had a name. True law aligns with justice; tyranny wears its mask but not its soul.

Nil difficile volenti
Nothing is difficult for the one who is willing.
The strength of will overcomes what strength of body cannot. Romans believed that desire, properly channeled, was a mighty engine.

O tempora! O mores!
Oh the times! Oh the morals!
Cicero's lament of decay and corruption. Every age believes itself fallen—this phrase captures Rome's own anxieties of decline.

Initium sapientiae timor domini
The beginning of wisdom is the fear of the gods.
To be wise is to know your limits. Romans may not have been religious in the modern sense, but they deeply respected higher powers.

Vox populi, vox Dei
The voice of the people is the voice of God.
An ancient recognition of democratic wisdom. When spoken with clarity, the will of the many could rival the will of heaven.

Victor est, qui victus fatetur
He is victorious who admits he has been defeated.
Humility is the final victory. To acknowledge loss is not to fall—but to rise in self-knowledge and grace.

Dies diem docet
One day teaches another.
Each day builds on the last. Time itself is a teacher, and wisdom unfolds not in revelation, but in accumulation.

About the Author

Maxwell W. Wilson is a passionate lifelong learner with a background in Information Technology and Contemporary Marketing. He believes that knowledge should be both enlightening and enjoyable—a philosophy he brings into every book he writes. For Maxwell, writing is more than just sharing information; it's about creating a journey where readers engage, learn, and have fun. His commitment to rigorous research ensures that every detail is spot-on, while his lively writing style keeps readers captivated. Whether you're diving into new concepts or brushing up on the familiar, Maxwell's books promise an experience that's both informative and refreshingly entertaining.

For a behind-the-scenes look at Maxwell's latest thoughts and projects, you can find him on Instagram under the handle **@anotsowiseoldman**.

Made in United States
Orlando, FL
02 July 2025

62551489R00022